SAMMY'S GLOBE-TROTTING ADVENTURES

It all started because . . .

I am a shepherd boy. I spend my days and nights roaming the hills, caring for my sheep. It is a lonely life. I miss having friends to talk with.

One of my lambs, Sammy, usually stays close by me. Sammy and I have become good friends. Talking to Sammy helps pass the time. I know that Sammy is just a sheep and cannot really understand what I am talking about. But he seems to listen very closely, almost as if he does understand.

Just the other day, I was telling Sammy about some of the exciting places God made in our world. It was fun describing oceans and jungles. Sammy has never seen a volcano or desert, so he enjoyed hearing what they are like.

While I was talking about these places, I told Sammy some of the ways that a good friend treats others. Of course, I know Sammy is a sheep, not a person, but he seemed to really want to learn how to treat others.

Maybe you would enjoy hearing some of the things I told Sammy. I would enjoy telling you. While you are learning, see if you can find Sammy and some of my other friends in the exciting pictures of different places in the world.

Illustrated by
Daniel J. Hochstatter

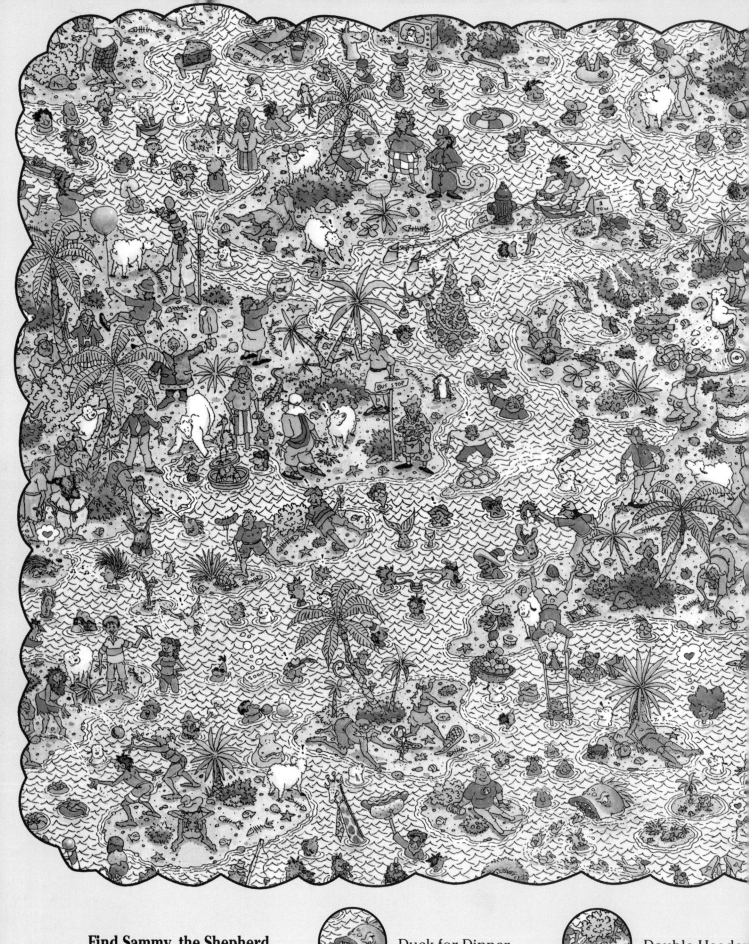

Find Sammy, the Shepherd, and as many of these things as you can.

 Duck for Dinner

 Double Header

 Sawfish

 Talented Turtle

TRUSTWORTHY TOMMY SAILS TO AN ISLAND

When a friend promises to meet you at a certain time, do you trust that person to be there? If you promise to keep a friend's secret, does your friend trust you?

It is important to have trustworthy friends. It is just as important to be the kind of friend who can be trusted. Trustworthy people can be depended on because they mean what they say. They are honest, and they keep their promises. Trustworthy people are more likely to have friends they can trust.

Trustworthy Tommy is the kind of friend who keeps his promises. He is enjoying a beautiful island. Can you find him?

Fishy Phone Call

Lemon Head

Trustworthy Tommy

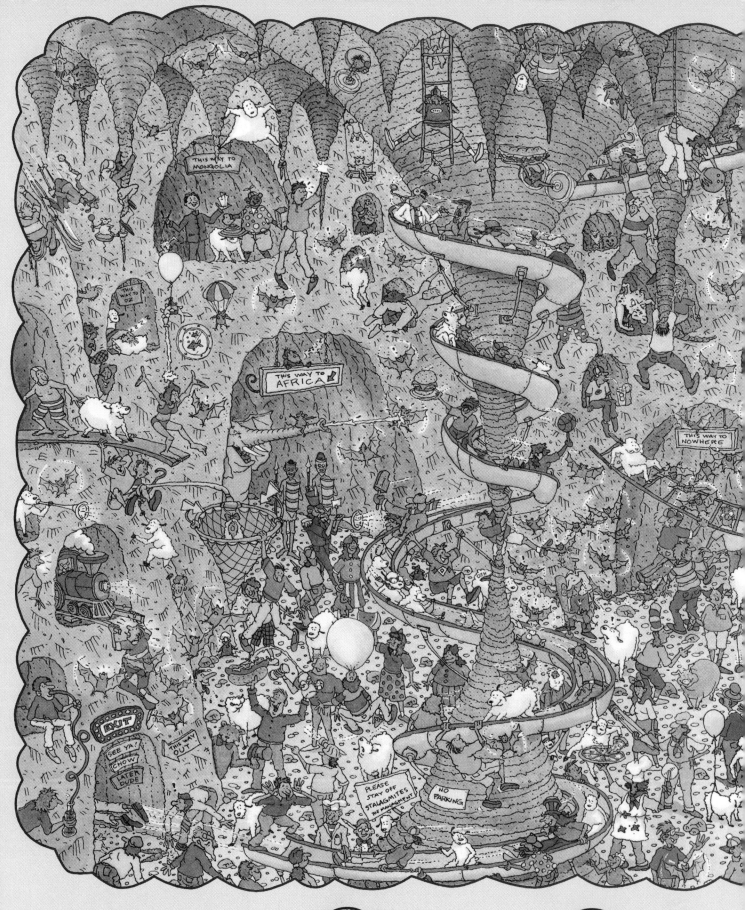

Find Sammy, the Shepherd, and as many of these things as you can.

 Fire Fighter

 Bowing Bear

 Say Aahhh!

 Catch of the Day

GRACIOUS GREG EXPLORES A CAVE

Gracious people are kind and polite. They speak with respectful voices. Gracious people do not treat others rudely. They make an effort to treat everyone fairly.

When gracious people win, they do not brag or gloat. If they lose, they congratulate the winners and really mean it! Gracious people take turns and play fairly. They are happy to let others go first.

Gracious Greg is exploring a cave. He shows he is gracious by waiting his turn crawling through tunnels and climbing over rocks. Can you find Greg?

Baseball Bat

Granny

Gracious Greg

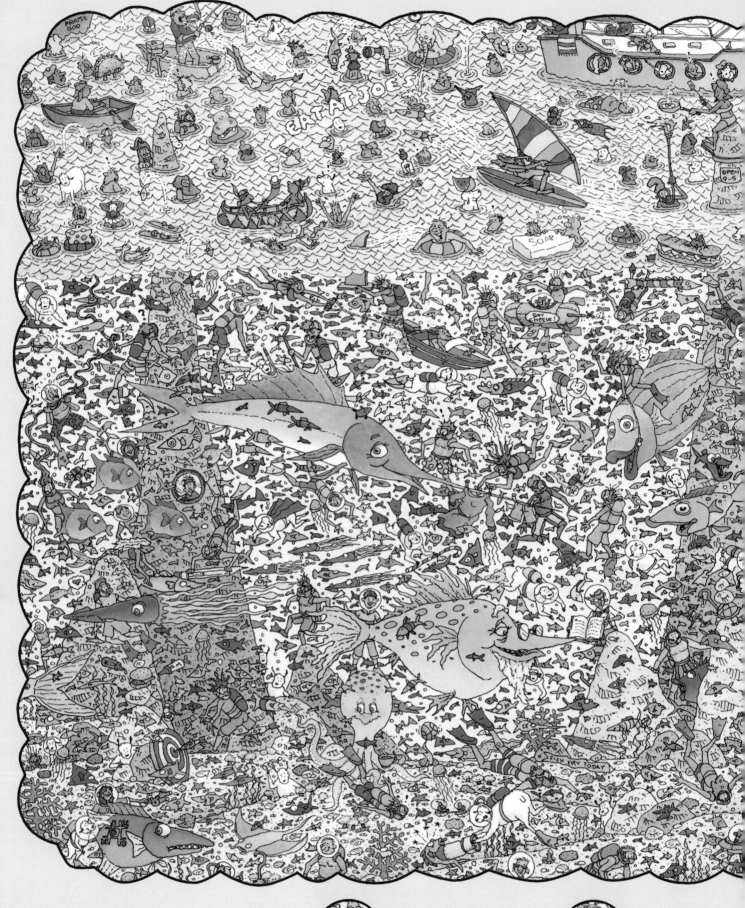

Find Sammy, the Shepherd, and as many of these things as you can.

 Funny–Face Fish

 Sub with Chee:

 Game Fish

 Lunching Lam

FRIENDLY FRANKIE SEARCHES AN OCEAN

It is easy to be friendly. Being friendly means taking time to talk with others. It means being interested in what they have to say. Friendly people want to know what is happening in others' lives.

People who are friendly do not talk with only their friends or people who are just like them. They also make friends with people who are different from them.

Friendly Frankie is discovering many different creatures in an ocean. Can you find him? He may be busy being friendly to someone who is not at all like him.

Seafood Taco

Jar of Jelly

Friendly Frankie

Find Sammy, the Shepherd, and as many of these things as you can.

 Amazing Baby

 B-Ball Bird

 Reduced Roadster

 Braidy Brenda

BRAVE BREANNA DISCOVERS A FOREST

Is there some situation that frightens you? Are you afraid of something you have to do or scared of something that could happen to you? You might be scared the first day you have to go to a new school. Or maybe you are afraid to ride on an airplane.

Brave people can overcome their fear when facing danger or something that is hard. They trust God to protect them and help them through every problem.

Brave Breanna is in a dark forest. The forest is full of strange sounds and scary animals. Brave Breanna is being very brave! Can you find her?

Party Sheep

Pleasured Porker

Brave Breanna

Find Sammy, the Shepherd, and as many of these things as you can.

 Braid and Bows

 Pasta Piggy

 Eskimo Joe

 Sharp Sheep

PERSISTENT PAM CLIMBS A MOUNTAIN

When you are looking for a favorite book or toy and it is not on the shelf where it should be, do you keep looking? If it is not under your bed or in the toy box, do you keep searching until you find it? That is persistence.

People who are persistent do not give up easily. Instead they keep working at whatever they are doing. Soon they find the lost book or toy or finish the job they were working on. Persistent people do not mind hard work. Their reward is a feeling of satisfaction when the job is finished.

Persistence is important for Persistent Pam. Climbing a mountain takes time and hard work. But the view from the top makes the persistence worthwhile. Can you find Pam on her way up this mountain?

Daddy Down Hill

Sherlock Sheep

Persistent Pam

Find Sammy, the Shepherd, and as many of these things as you can.

 Mousy Machine Operator

 Bird Buddy

 Peeking Porker

 Bubble–Gum Brenda

CARING CARRIE HIKES IN A JUNGLE

Caring people are concerned about how others feel. They understand when someone feels sad or hurt or lonely. Caring friends say and do things to help others.

People who are caring notice when a boy or girl is new to a group and has no one to talk with. They try to make everyone feel welcome. Caring people make others feel special and important by considering their feelings.

Caring Carrie is learning about the plants and animals in a jungle. Can you find her?

Tacky Tourister

Ranger Danger

Caring Carrie

Find Sammy, the Shepherd, and as many of these things as you can.

 Sheep Shooter

 Piggy Plunger

 Lemon Louie

 Shady Character

COMPASSIONATE KELLY RELAXES IN A FIELD

Compassion is caring, kindness, and generosity all rolled into one. Compassionate people feel sorry for those who are hurting. But they do not stop with just feeling sorry. They want to do something to help.

Compassionate people look for ways they can get involved with others. They are willing to give their time and energy to help someone else, even if it is not convenient for them.

Compassionate Kelly's friends know how caring she is. They are glad that she is relaxing in a field. Can you find her there?

Barbie Bumpy

Mustard Mess

Compassionate Kelly

Find Sammy, the Shepherd, and as many of these things as you can.

 Flying Carpet

 Hold Still

 Splitting Headache

 Bombs Away

GIVING GARY RAFTS DOWN A RIVER

Giving people make wonderful friends. They willingly give of their time, energy, talents, and possessions. Giving friends are happy to cut the grass for a sick neighbor or walk the dog for an older neighbor. They might give the last cookie in the bag to their friend. Giving people happily share their baseball and bat or favorite cars and dolls.

It is wonderful to have a giving friend, but it is also good to be a giving friend. Bringing happiness to other people makes giving people feel good, too.

Giving Gary is rafting down a river. Can you find Gary on his raft?

Toothache

Jailbreak

Giving Gary

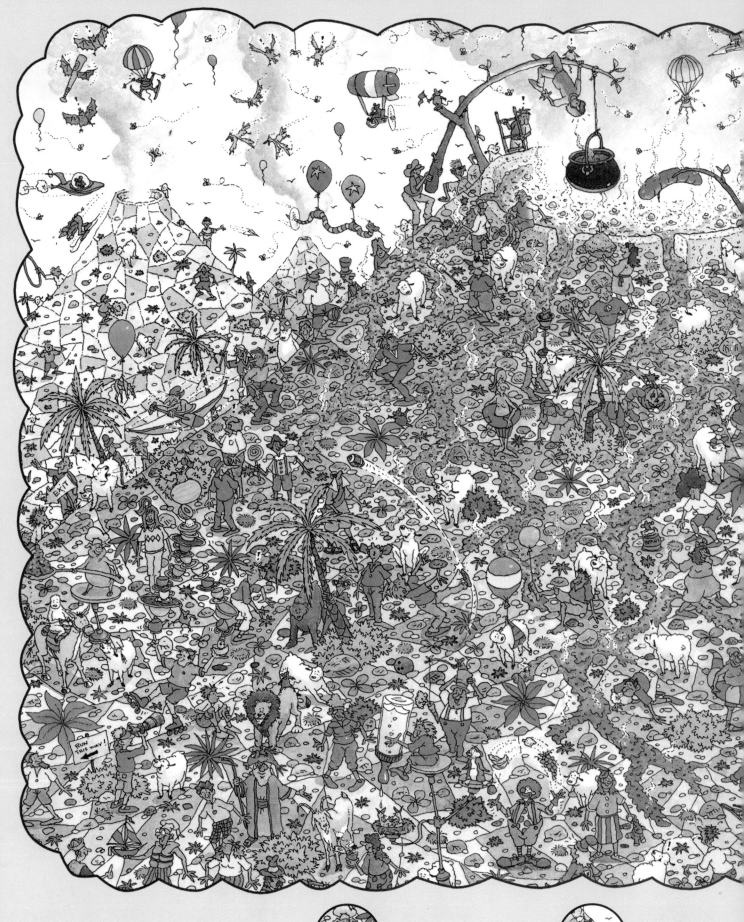

Find Sammy, the Shepherd, and as many of these things as you can.

 Porky Portion

 Pepperoni Picker

 Looking for the Lake

 Blue–Jay Pie

LOVING LAURA VIEWS A VOLCANO

Loving people are gentle and considerate. When others are sad, they help them feel better. They share happy times with their friends, too. Loving people look for ways to make others feel special.

Loving friends care about how others are feeling. Loving people know what is happening in their friends' lives. They look for ways they can help.

Loving Laura is impressed with the power of a big volcano. Can you find her?

Bacon Cheeseburger

Where's the Beach?

Loving Laura

Find Sammy, the Shepherd, and as many of these things as you can.

 Hats for Sale

 And...Action

 Raiding the Fridge

 What Goes Up.

POLITE PAULA SURVEYS A CANYON

Being polite means treating other people with respect. Polite people use a kind tone of voice. They remember to say please and thank you. They listen to what other people say. They do not ignore people or think others are unimportant. Polite people wait their turn and let others go first. Polite people sincerely try to treat others kindly.

Polite Paula is fascinated by the view of a canyon. Can you find her?

At the End of His Rope

Chopper Mouse

Polite Paula

Find Sammy, the Shepherd, and as many of these things as you can.

 Snake Mistake

 Beat the Heat

 Choked up

 Marty Martian

HAPPY HARVEY VIEWS A DESERT

Happy people are fun to be around. During a storm, they enjoy watching the rain instead of complaining about it. Happy people show pleasure with friends and with the world around them. Happy people make others feel good about the way things are going. They are content and are not frustrated by the ups and downs of life.

Happy Harvey can find things to be happy about, even in a desert. He does not think only about being hot and thirsty. He sees the beautiful plants and interesting animals. Can you find Harvey in the desert?

Hot Golfer

Popcorn Peddler

Happy Harvey

Find Sammy, the Shepherd, and as many of these things as you can.

 Frustrated Flosser

 Blow Fish

 Fly Boy

 Potential Headache

LOYAL LARRY
SKIS ON A
FROZEN TUNDRA

Have you ever heard someone making fun of one of your friends? What did you do? Did you join in?

Loyal people do not do that. They stand up for their friends. They are true to their friends. Loyal people are not influenced by others' opinions. Their friends know they can depend on them. Loyal friends are reliable friends.

Loyal Larry is skiing on a frozen tundra. Can you find him?

Muffski

Hare-I-Am

Loyal Larry

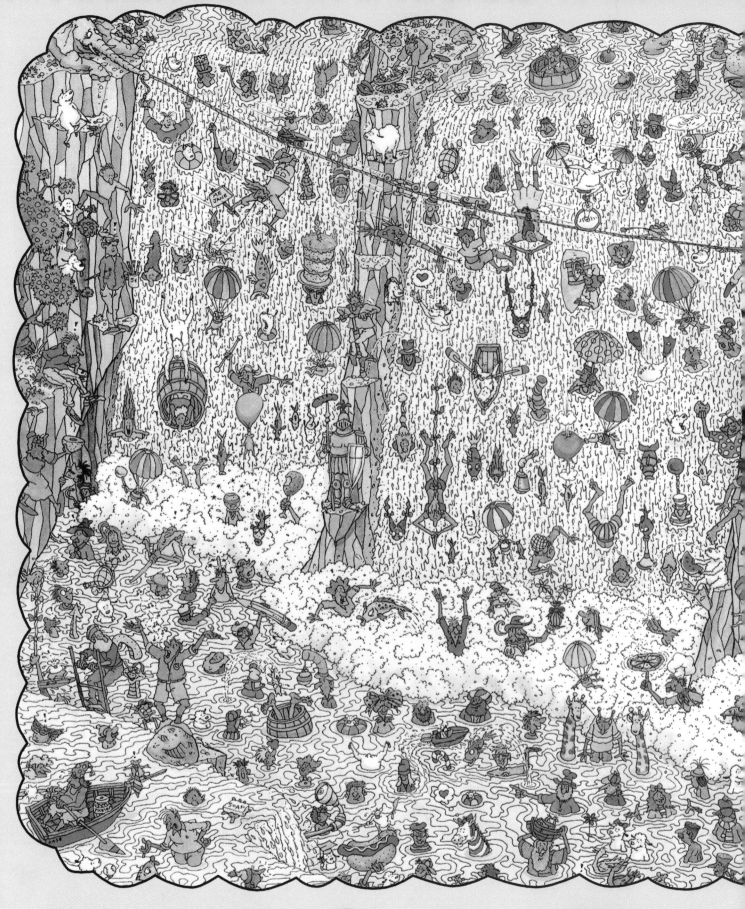

Find Sammy, the Shepherd, and as many of these things as you can.

 Party Sheep

 Noah

 Pencils for Sale

 Super Sandwich

THOUGHTFUL THEO ADMIRES A WATERFALL

Do you call or visit a friend who is feeling sad? Do you offer to go to the store for an older neighbor? Do you take time to play with a younger child so the child's parent can have a few minutes of rest? If you do these things or other things like them, you are thoughtful.

Thoughtful people look for ways to help others. They are willing to take the time and make the effort to be helpful and kind. Thoughtful people see ways to help others that other people do not even think of.

Thoughtful Theo is like that. He notices what is happening in other people's lives and he thinks about how he can help. Today Theo is enjoying the majesty of a waterfall. Can you find him?

Itsy Bitsy Bow

Ice–Pack Jack

Thoughtful Theo

Titles in
A Seeking Sammy Book
series:

**Sammy's Fantastic Journeys
with the
Early Heroes of the Bible**

**Sammy's Incredible Travels
with
Jesus and His Friends**

**Sammy's Excellent
Real-Life Adventures**

**Sammy's Tree-Mendous
Christmas Adventure**

**Sammy's Fabulous
Holy Land Travels**

**Sammy's Globe-Trotting
Adventures**

**Sammy's Big Book
of
Awesome Adventures**